Weather

by Lucy Long
illustrated by Nomar Perez

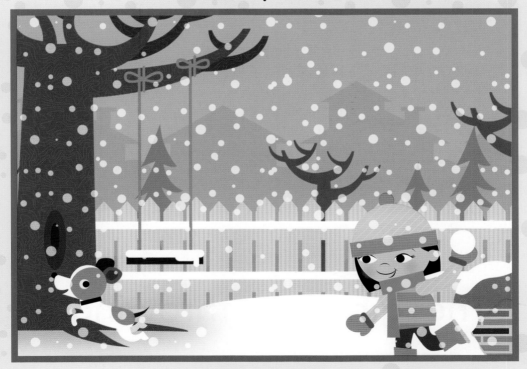

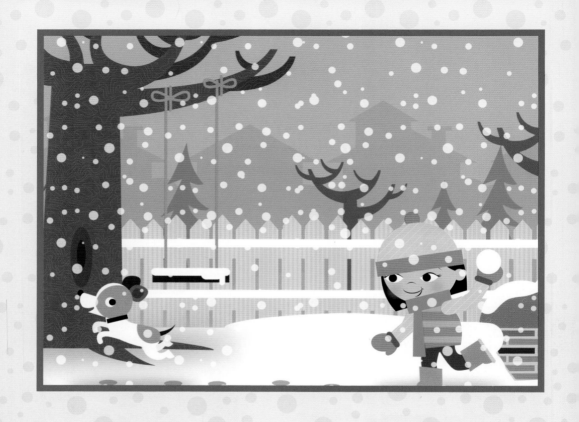

The girl was throwing.

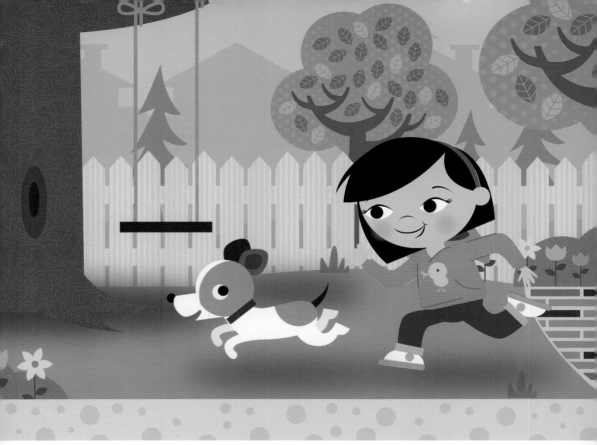

The girl was running.

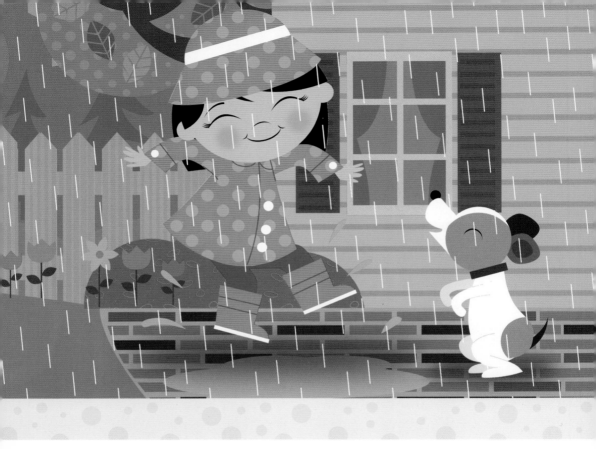

The girl was jumping.

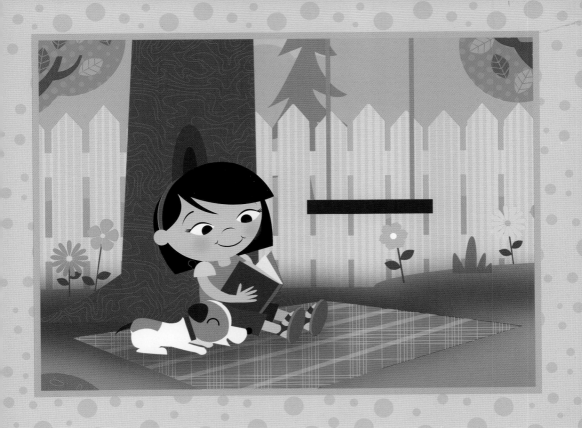

The girl was reading.

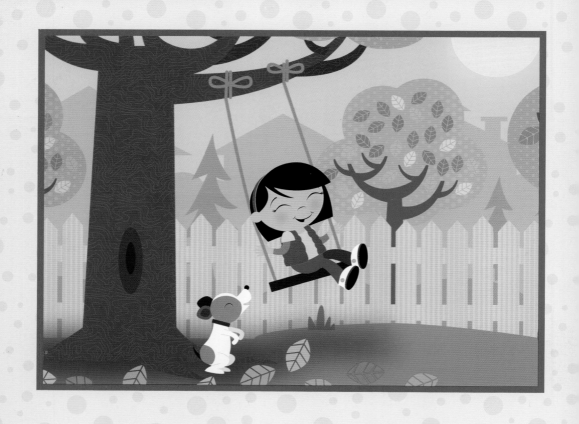

The girl was swinging.

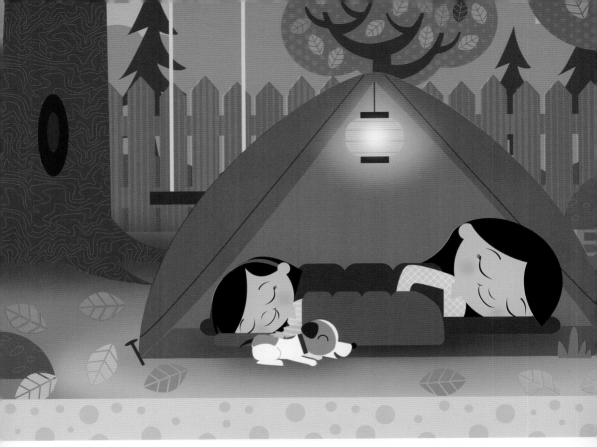

The girl was sleeping.

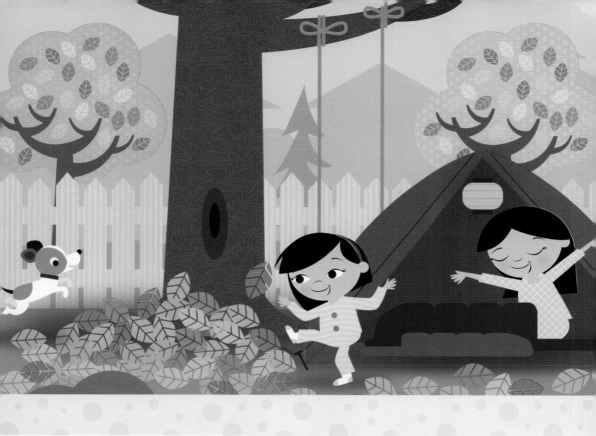

She was kicking!